CAMERA ABOVE THE CLOUDS

CAMERA ABOVE THE CLOUDS

The Aviation Photographs of Charles E. Brown

Edited by Anthony Harold

Airlife
England

ISBN 0 906393 31 0

First Published in 1983
by Airlife Publishing Ltd.

Airlife Publishing Ltd.

7 St. John's Hill, Shrewsbury, England.

Printed by Livesey Limited, Shrewsbury, England.

Foreword

by John Tanner, C.B.E., D.Litt., F.S.A., Director Royal Air Force Museums.

Experts have written that the art of photography has changed little since the camera was invented. Men of artistic vision at once used the new medium to capture exquisitely composed scenes, and portraits of penetrating understanding. However, the science and technology evolved rapidly, permitting a range of effects startling in their diversity and gripping in their intensity. Aerial photography was an immediate attraction to the pioneers and from the outset powered flight has challenged the photographers to give of their best.

There has not been, and probably never can be, a greater exponent of aviation photography than Charles E. Brown. He was a pioneer in the field, whose work, always outstanding, reached its full power and maturity in World War II, when his artistic sensibilities and technical prowess came perfectly together under the inspiration of the momentous era. Nothing was beyond him and no task found him wanting. He would fly at any time in any circumstances to capture the essence of the great flying machines of his time. When colour film was unobtainable, he obtained it — and it is largely thanks to him that the world knows the full glory of so many historic aircraft in the air. He combined technical skill with an acutely artistic eye. This book salutes his memory. The Royal Air Force Museum is proud to house his archive as one of the nation's aviation treasures.

Acknowledgements

The production of this book would not have been possible without the work of one man, Charles E. Brown. However, the task of bringing it to completion would not have been achieved without the foresight of the Aviation Records Department of the Royal Air Force Museum, who took the collection over, housed it and made my inconvenient researches possible. I would like to express my gratitude to the Director Dr. John Tanner CBE, Mr R. F. Barker, Mr R. Simpson, Mr R. Mack and Mr A. Cormack for their help and encouragement in the production of this edition.

I am very grateful for the interest and help that has been provided by Mrs Brown and Mrs G. Hawken, his daughter, who have kindly talked to me about Charles Brown and his work.

Francois Prins kindly supplied the photograph of the Palmos camera and his encouragement was much appreciated throughout the production of this book. Mr D. I. Roberts, also of the Royal Air Force Museum staff provided his invaluable help.

Charles E. Brown

Charles E. Brown was born on 20th January 1896, to Edward James Brown, a family butcher, whose business premises were in Arthur Road, Wimbledon Park. He was to become a pioneer and one of the most respected of all aviation photographers.

As a schoolboy he was lucky enough to be given a small folding camera for his fourteenth birthday, allowing him to explore the medium which was to shape his future.

Charles was slight of stature but clear headed and constructive in his attitudes. He lost no time in professionally exploiting that all important first newsworthy photograph, a balloon landing at Southfields, South London, one summer afternoon in 1911.

The photograph was presented to the *Daily Mirror* who duly paid him a half-guinea and published the picture. The art editor of that newspaper, Hannen Swaffer, was taken by the young Charles Brown and after discussing the picture with him asked if he would like to consider employment when he left school, with a view to press photography. Two years later Charles Brown left the LCC Central School and reminded the *Daily Mirror's* art editor of his promise. Charles Brown began work in the

Charles E. Brown: probably taken on the roof of the 'Daily Mirror', when at the age of 14 he was offered a job in the Photographic Department by Hannen Swaffer.

Charles Brown with his Palmos camera stands in the doorway of a DH Dragon Rapide.

Mirror's darkrooms under the guidance of Bernard Alferi (Senior); there he learned to process film and to print photographs.

As a fledgling press photographer he was justified in purchasing his own camera, a Zeiss Palmos fitted with a 6in Taylor Hobson helical focus lens; this purchase set him back the princely sum of £17. 15s. It is true to say that this camera was the greatest purchase of his life as most of his finest work was executed with it.

By the time war was declared in August 1914, the young Charles Brown was also being given photographic assignments, a role he would continue to enjoy for the rest of his working life. In 1915 he applied for a photographic posting with the Royal Naval Air Service, but was turned down by the Photographic Section and it seems he continued to work on photographic assignments wherever the newspaper sent him. Royal visits to factories and establishments were common; he even covered a Royal visit to Cranwell early in 1918 just before he achieved acceptance into the services.

He was drafted into the Royal Engineers and because of his medical category of B1 was posted to 532nd Agricultural Company Depot at Wrexham. His Certificate of Employment during the War records that he passed a trade test in photography with the Royal Engineers, as skilled, on the 10th August 1918. His number was 327968.

It appears that he was by then also doing work for the RAF at their London Photographic Centre in Hamilton Street, WC2 where he is recorded as being based from July 1918 until after 17th January 1919. Rail warrants and notices from the London Photographic Centre indicate that he undertook many official assignments during his time. He finally left military service on 17th January 1919 and rejoined his colleagues at the *Daily Mirror*.

In the post-war euphoria Alferi established his own press agency and Charles Brown went with him, quitting the *Mirror* offices for ever.

In 1921 Charles Brown started his own freelance press photography business, "Being my own boss is the only way I can do the work I enjoy" was the way he described his reasons later and his results certainly bear evidence of this wisdom.

Travel seems to have been an area in which he specialized, providing promotional material for all sorts of publicity purposes. He took many studies of locomotives which were eagerly accepted by the media. These pictures were however more than mere records; in each case he attempted to improve his skill, analyse composition, study light and generally improve his product.

He achieved great satisfaction from the success one of his photographs enjoyed. On platform 4 at Waterloo he photographed a small boy in conversation with the driver of a Southern Railway express locomotive.

The faithful Palmos camera.

Ready for one of his last assignments at Lasham in an Auster 6.

This simple image was to feature for more than ten years in the Southern Railway's advertising campaigns. In the early thirties it was impossible to read the slogan 'South for Sunshine' without seeing the work of Charles Brown.

The success of this one picture made it easier for him to diversify. Aeroplanes were a good source of news interest as the developments and achievements in that field took the public imagination. He began his aeronautical collection by photographing at RAF stations and air displays like the annual Hendon meeting. The close proximity of Croydon was not to be overlooked as he was resident in the Wimbledon Park/Worcester Park area all his life.

His growing acclaim through the sale of aircraft photographs led to him being invited to fly in the tail turret of a Vickers Virginia bomber. For the first time he experienced the full challenge of air to air photography, the field in which he was to excel. For the remaining years of the uneasy peace which terminated finally in 1939, he flew with many squadrons of the Royal Air Force and with the Fleet Air Arm. Access to military aviation was possible through the press division of the Admiralty, headed by Captain Clarke and through Charles Robertson of the Air Ministry Public Relations department. With the help of these departments Charles Brown was able to get every assistance he required for his photographic assignments. From the letters which he kept, it is obvious that airmen enjoyed working for him and Charles Brown in turn was always thoughtful enough to send copies of his photographs to those who had helped. Developments in the aviation industry would inevitably lead to a commission to photograph a company's latest product; all newsworthy aviation topics were his assignments and he enjoyed many official press invitations.

At this time, there were two influential photographers also in the aviation field, John Yoxall and Charles Simms. Both worked for journals that required quick results and exclusive rights on their photographs. This tied situation often restricted the distribution of the very fine photographs both produced. Charles Brown, an independent, not only enjoyed exclusive use of aeroplanes for his work but freedom to exploit his photographs to a larger media coverage and with the increased development of all types of aircraft there was plenty of work for all.

His growing reputation for magnificent aviation photographs ensured that wherever he went he was given the best possible opportunities to take his pictures. This meant that on a visit to the Fleet he would get the better pilots flying for him, and would be given almost unlimited facilities in flying time and effort for him to achieve the best results. In retrospect this happily guaranteed an almost unique record of aircraft in flight from 1923 until he quietly retired in the 60's.

He enjoyed a rich harvest of aeronautical studies before the start of the Second World War. He took on photographic assignments in the Middle

Charles Brown prepares to photograph aircraft taking part in the 1953 SBAC airshow.

East, in the Mediterranean and for various tourist organisations, enjoyed skiing and working holidays in the fashionable Alpine resorts like St. Moritz and Wengen.

When asked which was his favourite picture, he replied, "There have been too many". Having looked through several thousand prints for this book, I know exactly what he means. But the photograph he was most pleased with was his superb picture of three No. 87 Squadron Gladiators, whilst the picture that brought him the most income was the study of the Fairey Seal which is reproduced on page 49.

When war broke out he was still in business in Shoe Lane and the collection of photographs had reached considerable proportions, some 25,000 negatives. Like many citizens who had already been in one war and were strictly speaking too old for active service, he volunteered to help the local community by becoming an ARP warden.

During the Blitz, in the winter of 1940/41, he returned from a photographic assignment in the West Country to find that his Fleet Street premises had been the inadvertent target of a German bomb. Many priceless negatives were shattered. Many more were boxed together and moved successfully to premises in 14 Longfellow Road, Worcester Park, where his business remained until the mid-seventies. At this time, he carried out a great deal of work for the magazine *Aeronautics* which was edited by Oliver Stewart. Each edition was lavishly illustrated with Charles Brown's photographs, some of which were in colour.

A little later in the war he was made an official war correspondent and again, in connection with his appointment, was sent in 1944 to cover

The photographer photographed at work – 1953 SBAC airshow.

aspects of the work of the 2nd Tactical Air Force in their progress through recently occupied Europe. On these assignments he tended to use his 35mm Zeiss Contax camera which he purchased in 1935, in preference to the large format Palmos.

During the last war colour film stock was made available by American agencies and approached by *Flying,* he took up assignments for that magazine ensuring that he obtained a supply of the coveted Kodachrome and Ektachrome film. His colour photographs of aircraft during World War II are now a tremendously important and valuable collection. Many of the photographs he took were sent to the editor of *Flying,* W. B. Ziff, who only returned transparencies he did not wish to publish, and so a complete collection of his colour work probably no longer exists.

He used his colour film resources with great care; it seems he rarely exposed more than three transparencies on any one subject, and indeed probably only twice that number in black and white. This stringent economy left very little room for errors and in fact few were made. His insistence that he photographed as much as possible with a clear view and without cockpit panels and perspex fairings, which distorted the camera's view, became an increasing problem as the speed and efficiency of aircraft increased. He managed to photograph most Allied aircraft types during the last war and not surprisingly he found himself, at times, back with the Navy to capture on film the latest developments including Lease Lend arrivals. The Lancaster and similar multi-engined aircraft provided camera platforms and the close-up pictures he took from their tail turrets are amongst the finest technical photographs in his collection.

In the bustling peace that happily succeeded the war in Europe, he was kept busy on assignments by the aircraft industry. Many new designs were being produced and he was invited by the big companies to provide them with first class images. No expense was spared and he would spend hours airborne looking for the right location and cloud effects. His photographs of the prototype Hastings were so clear that on appraisal of his results the design team noticed that the undercarriage doors were not completely closing. They examined the aircraft and found a design fault which was rectified. If the photographs had not been of such a high quality it could have taken them months to discover the problem.

Flying with experienced and well known aviators and test pilots he logged some 3,000 hours in the air without a significant incident. He has left a unique record of production aircraft and important prototypes from the early jet age.

His great talent was recognised by his peers on a number of occasions, both with awards for photographic ability and through the invitation to exhibit his work. As early as 1938 the Ilford Galleries put on an exhibition entitled *Life in the Royal Air Force* which featured forty of his best photographs and one of his last exhibitions was for Kodak. He was awarded the Charles Robertson Trophy for his work in the portrayal of the Royal Air Force to the public. The Royal Photographic Society made

Charles Brown (left) briefs the crew of a Bristol Freighter before an assignment.

him a Fellow and he was also a Fellow of the Institute of Incorporated Photographers.

I first met him in 1972 and although it was obvious that his health was a severe handicap, he kindly came to his old business premises in Longfellow Road to supply me with some photographs for the Royal Air Force Museum. He reminisced about many of the photographs in his collection, the happy memories of his days with the Fleet at Gibraltar, his success with the Southern Railway, a print of which hung on a wall and so forth, but he could not really face the problems posed by his massive collection. The weight of glass in negative form was a structural worry, the damp was likely to damage his precious images and the boxed negatives rescued from the Shoe Lane office remained unsorted.

His life's work was threatened and it was with great relief to all who were concerned that he finally agreed to allow his entire collection to be purchased by the Royal Air Force Museum. His hopes of administering his business from home were never realized and although he never retired, he lived in his old home in Delta Road, isolated from his achievements.

In 1978 the collection in its entirety was successfully moved to Hendon where it is being slowly and carefully catalogued and restored.

As the collection left for Hendon, he moved happily into the RAF home at Storrington. Living amongst his memories he was happy. On 9th October 1982, Charles E. Brown died. The man may have gone but his spirit will endure through the thousands of images he has left us to enjoy.

1919 - 1939

In 1918 the Great War came to an end and a massive run down of manufacturing and man-power began. In the flying world, thousands of pilots were demobbed and the Royal Air Force, in 1919, began to shrink to a mere shadow of its wartime strength. For that service the war, however, would not end for in the Middle and Far East, disputes between local potentates would keep the Air Force busy, 'keeping the peace,' for many years. At home a handful of fighter squadrons were kept for home defence whilst the bomber was given preference as an offensive weapon.

Civil aviation developed quickly, initially using ex-military aircraft so that by the early thirties new aeroplanes were being designed and constructed for every conceivable purpose. In 1931 the Schneider Trophy seaplanes had achieved speeds in excess of 400 mph and record breaking and non-stop flights to all parts of the Empire had been accomplished.

In 1934, alarmed by the political situation in Europe, the Air Ministry began the expansion of the RAF and in the years leading up to the Second World War in September 1939, development of aircraft and the training of crews became a national priority. The beautiful biplanes gave way in what became known as the expansion period to camouflaged monoplanes of sinister aspect. Fighters developed into fast, heavily armed monoplanes and the airman became less a craftsman, more a technologist.

Charles Brown began to get established in and to concentrate on aviation from the late twenties and provided thereafter a superb record of the development of aviation in the flying services of the Empire.

MONSIEUR MIGNET'S GLIDER
One of the earliest aviation photographs taken by Charles E. Brown is this lovely study on the beach at Veauville in Normandy. The ladies are trying to get one of Monsieur Mignet's gliders airborne on what proved to be a calm afternoon in August 1923.

FAIREY FLYCATCHER I

A Fairey Flycatcher I, N9928 of No. 403 Flight based on board *HMS Hermes.*

The Flycatcher was unmistakable in its character and aroused great affection in the pilots who flew the little fighters.

Powered by two variants of the Armstrong Siddeley Jaguar III or IV and armed with two synchronised .303 machine guns, the Flycatcher was capable of 133 mph at 5,000 feet.

Design work began in 1922 and the Flycatcher entered service in 1923. It remained a front line fighter until 1934.

MAINTENANCE
Servicing the Armstrong Siddeley Jaguar engines of an Armstrong Whitworth Argosy I at Croydon in 1929.

SUPERMARINE SOUTHAMPTON II

The first flying boat designed after WWI, to enter service with the RAF the Southampton was issued in 1925 to what became No. 201 Squadron. There were 78 delivered to the service which used the type until it was superseded in 1935. The RAF carried out several historic flights with these aeroplanes, the most memorable being the 27,000 mile cruise by the Far East Flight of four aircraft in 1927.

This photograph shows two Southampton Mk IIs near Cowes, Isle of Wight.

SHORT S8 CALCUTTA
The Short S8 Calcutta was first flown by J. Lankester Parker in February 1928. Its trials were satisfactory and G-EBUG, the first of two aircraft ordered, was accepted by Imperial Airways.
It was landed on the Thames at Westminster and was inspected by Members of Parliament. It was important that it was understood that this relatively large aeroplane was part of a link which would carry passengers the length and breadth of the British Empire.
Powered by 3 Bristol Jupiter XIF radials, the Calcutta was the first flying boat with a stressed skin metal hull to enter commercial service. Its wing span was 97 feet.

ARMSTRONG WHITWORTH ARGOSY I

One of the great airliners in use with Imperial Airways, the Armstrong Whitworth Argosy I. Here G-EBLF flies from Croydon out over London, circa 1929.

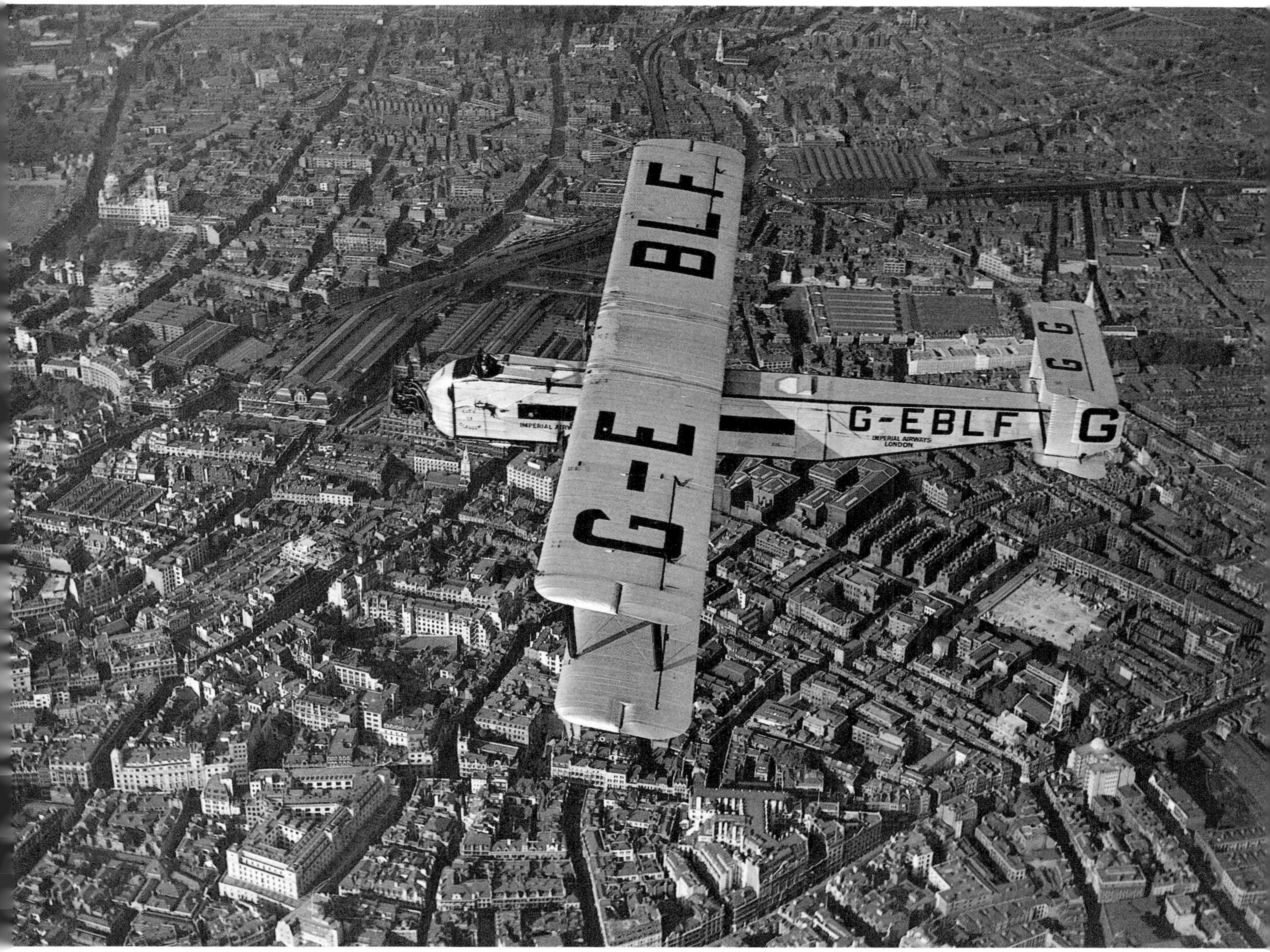

TIGER MOTH Mk.I *(opposite)*
Instructors from the Central Flying School practise formation aerobatics prior to the Hendon Air Display of 1932.
The aircraft are Tiger Moth Mk.I's from the first production batch. These aeroplanes, K2583-87, were specially modified for inverted flight and for visual effect the top surfaces of all wings were painted with red and white chequers.
At this time training aircraft were finished in the ubiquitous silver paint with black serial numbers. The use of yellow as a training colour was soon to be adopted.

RYAN
The aftermath of Charles Lindberg's historic solo crossing of the Atlantic on the 21 May 1927.
Charles Brown took this photograph of Lindberg's NYP (New York to Paris) Ryan whilst it was under guard at Paris.
Tears in the fabric, made by the over enthusiastic crowds, can clearly be seen.
The flight carried out by Charles Lindberg, then aged twenty five, took 33½ hours and covered a distance of 3,610 miles.
The young aviator claimed the prize of $25,000 and became a national hero literally overnight.

DH60M GIPSY MOTH *(opposite)*
Refuelling a DH60M Gipsy Moth, one of 78 built for the RAF as communications aircraft.

BRISTOL FIGHTER Mk.IV
In July 1928 the Oxford and Cambridge University Air Squadrons became equipped with the final version of the Bristol Fighter, the Mk.IV.
The Bristol Fighter, Bristol type 96, became a formidable fighter aircraft on the Western front in 1918 and continued with various modifications to provide the RAF with a versatile fighting aircraft in the Middle East. The 'Brisfit' was finally replaced in overseas service by Westland Wapitis in 1931.
J8257 is a Mk.IV dual control trainer issued to Oxford U.A.S. featuring the Handley Page slots and a modified horn-balance rudder and cambered fin.

FAIREY FIREFLY Mk.III
In their efforts to provide the RAF with a potent fighter the Fairey company developed the Firefly. Its design, first conceived in 1924, was based on the streamline advantages of the V-12 engine. In its final form, Mk.III, the little aeroplane was capable of 188 mph at sea level.
S1592 is photographed in July 1932 as a landplane. Some of its career was spent on floats as a seaplane trainer for the RAF Schneider Trophy team at Calshot in 1931. The type never achieved production orders from the Air Ministry although the Mk.III was designed specifically to provide a single-seater deck-landing fighter. It first flew in May 1929.

DE HAVILLAND DH84 DRAGON
A magnificent photograph of a de Havilland DH84 Dragon.

WESTLAND WAPITI
Westland Wapitis of No. 601 Squadron Royal Auxiliary Air Force cruise gently over the English countryside. The Wapiti, designed as a replacement for the DH9, first flew in 1927. Many of the 517 aircraft were to be used overseas in the Middle East and India, however, in October 1929 the first Auxiliary Squadron, No. 600, was equipped with the type.
Wapitis were designed as general purpose aircraft of metal construction. The type equipped several squadrons in India, three squadrons in Iraq and became the initial equipment of ten Royal Auxiliary Squadrons in whose service the type was finally retired in 1937.

HAWKER HART
In 1928 the first Hawker Hart, a two-seater light bomber, flew and successfully gained Air Ministry production orders. It was to become a widely used type from 1930, when the first Squadron, No. 33, received Harts, until 1939 when the last were replaced, on the North West frontier, by Bristol Blenheims.

TIGER MOTH DH82A
Fitted with a 130 hp de Havilland Gipsy Major engine and a plywood rear fuselage decking, the Tiger Moth achieved a new designation, the DH82A.
The first of many civil registered Tiger Moths was G-ACDA, constructed at Martlesham Heath in 1933. Following its trials the type was allocated to civilian operated Elementary and Reserve Flying Schools which were intended to provide *ab initio* training for RAF pilots. Nine schools used the Tiger Moth in civil markings, No. 1 being the de Havilland School of Flying Ltd., based at Hatfield. This photograph shows the first Tigers of the first school in formation. The livery was dark red and silver.

AVRO TUTOR
The tradition set by the instructors of the Central Flying School performing precision aerobatic formation flying continued for many years. Avro Tutors were adopted in 1933 and in subsequent shows were adorned with red and white sun rays painted on the upper mainplanes.
K3363 was initially issued to C.F.S. and was finally sold in November 1946.

AVRO TUTOR
Avro Tutors of the Central Flying School at practise for the 1933 RAF Hendon Air Display.
The Tutor was ordered into service in 1931 and a total of 400 were built for the RAF. Powered by an Armstrong Siddeley Lynx IVc radial engine the aeroplane proved to be a most satisfactory elementary trainer. Production of the type ceased in 1936.

BRISTOL BULLDOG IIA
Bristol Bulldog IIAs of No. 32 Squadron, based at Biggin Hill close in on the camera aircraft.
Bulldogs were the mainstay of the UK fighter defence from 1929 to 1935 and equipped ten squadrons, giving way to the more advanced Gloster Gauntlet and Gladiator fighters.
The Bulldogs in this photograph have been modified and are now fitted with brakes, a tail wheel, a modified fin and full night flying equipment.
No. 32 Squadron finally gave up their Bulldogs in July 1936.

HAWKER DEMON

The remarkable performance of the Hawker Hart forced the Air Ministry to order an appropriate variant to act as a fighter. The resulting two-seater fighter became known as the Hawker Demon in 1932.

The first Squadron to receive the type was No. 23 Squadron in 1931 when enough aircraft to equip one flight were provided. The experiment was successful and led to the adoption of the type in 15 fighter squadrons of the RAF.

Demon K5740 was built by Boulton Paul at Wolverhampton and was one of a small batch fitted with a Frazer-Nash hydraulic turret. The Rolls-Royce Kestrel (DC) V engine provided 560 hp which gave the Demon a top speed of 182 mph at 16,500 feet.

Hawker Demons became obsolete by 1939, many being replaced by the Bristol Blenheim.

AVRO TUTORS
Instructors and pupils prepare for an afternoon's flying with the University of London Air Squadron. The Avro Tutors were collected from a variety of units, K3391 was sent from No. 6 Flying Training School, whilst K3453 in the foreground was issued new to ULAS.

GLOSTER GAUNTLET
Gloster Gauntlet fighters of No. 19 Squadron. The first Gauntlets to enter RAF service replaced Bristol Bulldogs in 19 Squadron based at Duxford. The squadron was fully equipped with the type by May 1935.

SUPERMARINE SCAPA *(opposite)*
The Supermarine Scapa, a re-engined and improved Southampton, first flew in 1932 and was finally withdrawn from RAF service in 1938. The type equipped only two squadrons, No. 202 in Malta and No. 240 Squadron based at Calshot on the Solent. The Scapa was a general reconnaissance flying boat with an all metal airframe, Rolls-Royce Kestrel engines and a crew of five.

GLOSTER GAUNTLET I
A flight of three Gloster Gauntlet I fighters over Cambridgeshire in 1935. The type was to become one of the best liked biplane fighters of the inter-war period.

VICKERS VALENTIA

Vickers Valentias flying sedately above the sands of Egypt. Two squadrons, No. 70 & No. 216, flew the type from 1934 until they were replaced by Vickers Wellingtons and Bristol Bombays respectively.

The aircraft had accommodation for 22 troops plus 3 crew. They were also capable of carrying a 2,200 lb bomb load attached to racks below the wings. With their two Bristol Pegasus engines these ungainly aircraft could achieve 130 mph at 5,000 feet.

THE VICKERS VIRGINIA
The Vickers Virginia was one of the mainstays of the inter-war bomber force, remaining in service from 1924 until 1937.
This photograph is taken from the rear gunner's position looking forward to reveal the birdcage of struts and wires on this No. 7 Squadron Virginia X.
A total of 126 Virginias were completed when production ceased late in 1932.

BRISTOL BULLDOG

Bristol Bulldogs of No. 3 Squadron, based at Kenley, prepare for their formation aerobatic participation in the 1935 Royal Air Force Display at Hendon.

No. 3 Squadron was the unit chosen to introduce the Bulldog into service, their first aircraft arriving in June 1929. The Squadron was, significantly, one of the last to operate the type; their late MkIIAs were sent to the Sudan during the Abyssinian crisis, returning after 11 months to the UK in August 1936.

One year later the Bulldogs were replaced by Gloster Gladiators which also inherited the emerald green stripes that were the official squadron markings.

HAWKER OSPREY
Fitters work in the Mediterranean heat on the engine of a Hawker Osprey.

VICKERS VIRGINIA
Vickers Virginia Xs of No. 7 Squadron.

ARMSTRONG WHITWORTH ATLAS

The Armstrong Whitworth Atlas was designed as an army co-operation aircraft and in this role it saw service with nine squadrons of the RAF.

The first aircraft entered service in 1927 and dual controlled training versions became available from 1931. They were superseded by Hart Trainers in 1935.

K-1175 was a two-seater Atlas trainer.

BOULTON PAUL OVERSTRAND

The Boulton Paul Overstrand was a curious looking bomber which was one of the first to be fitted with glazed gun turrets. The type was only allocated to one squadron, No. 101, which flew the type from 1935 to 1938 when they were based at Bicester.

HAWKER HART TRAINER
Learning to fly in style! The Hawker Hart Trainer was essentially similar to the Hart Light Bomber with the removal of the gun mounting and its replacement with a rear cockpit and dual controls.
It made a great deal of sense producing a training aircraft which was akin to current service machinery.
The Hart Trainer first flew in 1932 and provided valuable service until 1939 when it was superseded by the Harvard and Master.
K6450 was a Hart Trainer built by Armstrong Whitworth in 1936. It was issued to No. 1 School of Technical Training, No. 10 Elementary & Reserve Flying Training School and the Royal Air Force College Cranwell, being finally sent to the South African Air Force in 1942.

FAIREY SWORDFISH

A Fairey Swordfish, L2742 of No. 701 Catapult Flight flies past the southern tip of Gibraltar in the carefree days preceding the Second World war.

FAIREY SEAL *(opposite)*
Charles Brown enjoyed his assignments with the Royal Navy in the Mediterranean. On one such occasion he took this photograph of a Fairey Seal, the Naval version of the Gordon, flying over a destroyer flotilla with the great Rock of Gibraltar in the background. K4201 was struck off charge on 22nd March 1938.

FAIREY SEAL
A Fairey Seal landing on the flight deck of *HMS Courageous* whilst serving with No. 820 Squadron. This aeroplane, K3481, was constructed early in 1933 and served with five units before being written off in a crash at Usworth in 1939.
The Fairey Seal was a three-seater land or seaplane, powered by an Armstrong Siddeley Panther IIa radial engine and represented the final development of the Fairey III series of spotter reconnaissance aircraft, which were the most widely used aircraft in the Fleet Air Arm.

K4207
735

FAIREY BATTLE
The prototype Fairey Battle flies over the flight hangar on the corner of the Great West aerodrome which later became Heathrow.
K4303 first flew on the 10th of March 1936 and this photograph, showing the aeroplane in its earliest form must have been taken shortly after.
The Battle was powered by a Rolls-Royce Merlin I and it was to equip the production Battle that the Merlin was first ordered.
The Battle was designed to Air Ministry specification P.27/32 for a light bomber to replace the Hawker Hart then in service.

HAWKER DEMONS OF No. 604 SQUADRON
In 1934 No. 604 Auxiliary squadron, recently formed as a light bomber squadron, received fighter status. Its first aeroplanes were Hawker Demons, variants of the Hart bomber which proved faster than most single-seater fighters of the time. The photograph was taken shortly after the squadron received its Demons which they kept until 1939 when they were replaced by Blenheim Is.

K
6206
K6206
220

AVRO ANSON *(opposite)*
The Avro Anson, type 652a, first flew in prototype form in 1935. The Anson demonstrated its superior range and endurance at the Coastal Defence Development Unit at Gosport and was ordered in quantity by the Air Ministry. The first aircraft of that production order were delivered in early 1936.
Anson K6206, photographed here flying over *HMS Revenge,* belonged to No. 220 Squadron which reformed with the aircraft at Bircham Newton in August 1936.
The Anson was replaced in No. 220 Squadron by the Lockheed Hudson in September 1939.

HAWKER HURRICANE
A superb study of the prototype Hawker Hurricane K5083 in flight. On 6th November 1935, George Bullman made the first test flight of the aeroplane which was to play such an important role in the future course of aerial warfare.

MILES KESTREL TRAINER M.9

The Miles Kestrel Trainer M.9 was a truly brilliant design and a new departure for Miles Aircraft. Fitted with a Rolls-Royce Kestrel XVI engine which gave the aircraft a top speed of 296 mph at 14,000 feet, the company had really succeeded in the realms of high powered flight. Further development created the Master I, which became a standard advanced trainer for the RAF.

The photograph illustrates the Kestrel flying just before or just after the 1937 Hendon Air Display. Its new type number 2 is prominently displayed.

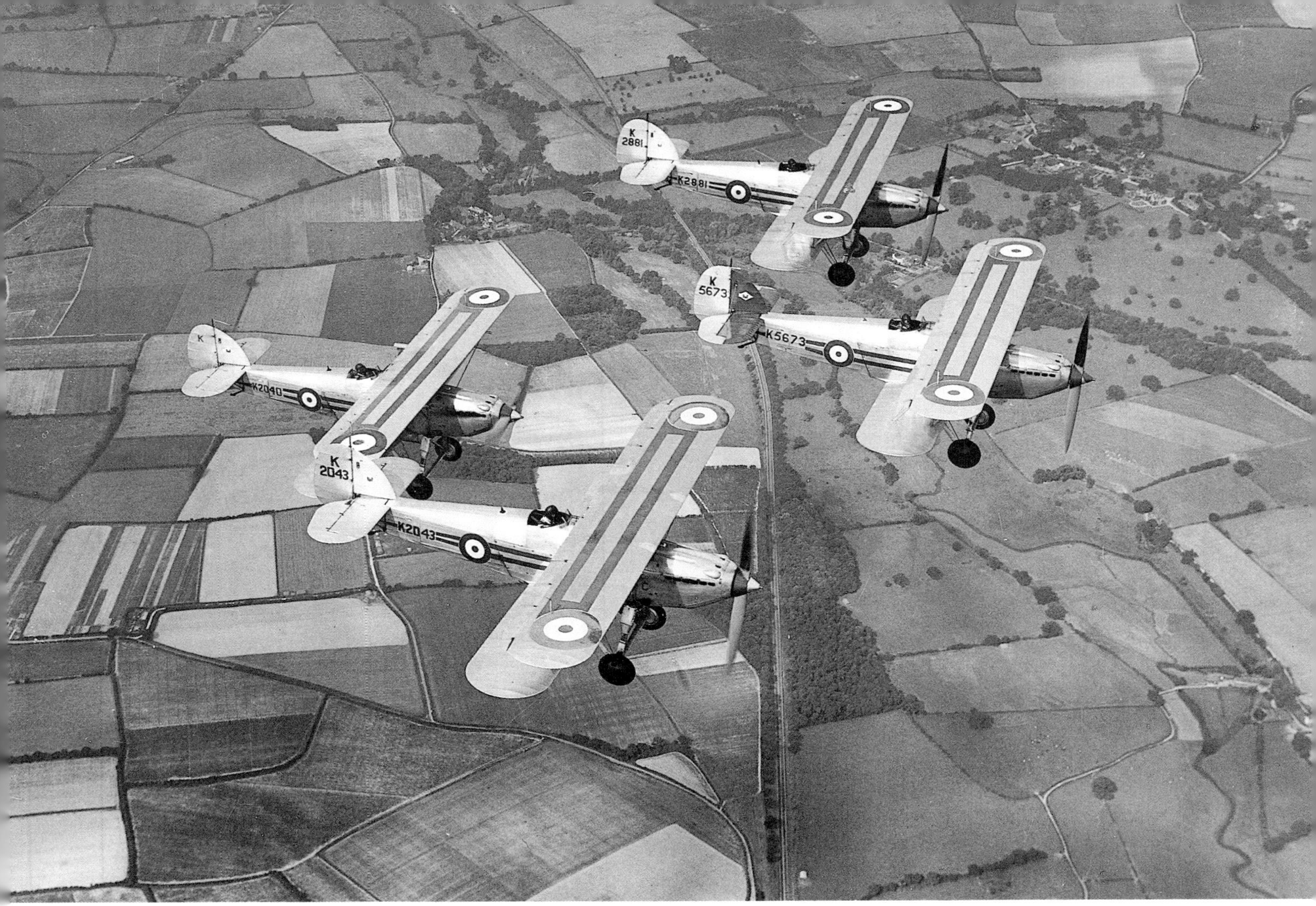

HAWKER FURY
The four aircraft team of No. 1 Squadron in 1937. The Hawker Fury was considered by many to be the most attractive aeroplane of the inter-war period. It was the first RAF fighter to exceed 200 mph. Principally only used by three fighter squadrons, the Fury entered service in 1931 with Nos. 1, 25 and 43 Squadrons.

NO. 1 SQUADRON AEROBATIC TEAM
In 1937 the formation aerobatic team at No. 1 Squadron were chosen after competition with Nos. 3 and 59 Squadrons to represent the RAF at various air shows, including the RAF Display at Hendon.
The members of the team were Flight Lieutenant E. M. Donaldson, Flying Officer H. E. C. Boxer and Pilot Officers P. R. Walker and P. P. Harks.

AEROBATIC GLOSTER GLADIATORS
Gloster Gladiators of No. 87 Squadron demonstrate their prowess in tied together aerobatics high over Debden during the summer of 1938.
This trio represented the Royal Air Force at the prestigious Villacoublay Air Show in France on 10th July 1938.

PILOTS OF THE GLOSTER GLADIATORS
The pilots of 87 Squadron who flew the tied together formation aerobatics in 1938. They are: Flying Officer G. H. J. Fearny, Pilot Officer R. L. Lorimer and Sergeant Dewdrey.

HAWKER HURRICANE I

Hawker Hurricane I's of No. 111 Squadron flying from Northolt in 1938. Delivery of the production Hurricane began in December 1937. No. 111 Squadron was the first to be equipped with the new monoplane fighter. The lead aircraft in the first 'Vic' is flown by Squadron Leader Gillan who, in this aircraft, achieved an average speed of 408 mph for the 327 miles between Turnhouse and Northolt. Two years later No. 111 Squadron was to play a significant part in the Battle of Britain, still equipped with Hurricanes.

FAIREY BATTLE
A fine study of a Fairey Battle as the type became introduced into squadron service. Battle K7650 was built at Stockport by Fairey Aviation and was delivered to No. 463 Squadron, based at Upwood in Huntingdonshire. This photograph was probably taken early in 1938.

VICKERS WELLESLEY

First built as a private venture by Vickers, the Wellesley became the first aircraft to enter RAF service utilizing the Geodetic Construction, employed so successfully in their next design, the Wellington.

Designed as a general purpose bomber, the Wellesley, powered by a 925 hp Bristol Pegasus engine, could carry a maximum bomb load of 2,000 lb some 1,110 miles at 188 mph.

The Wellesley equipped 5 home based squadrons and 4 overseas squadrons between April 1937 when the type entered service with No. 76 Squadron and retirement, overseas, in 1941.

The three aircraft pictured are from the RAF Long-Range Development Flight. On 5th November 1938 these three aircraft left Ismailia in Egypt to fly to Darwin, non-stop. Two of the three aircraft arrived safely, flying 7,162 miles in under 48 hours.

Provision was made on these aircraft for a third crewman and extra fuel.

ARMSTRONG WHITWORTH WHITLEY MkI AND MkIV

The prototype Whitley bomber flew on 17th March 1936 and was ordered into production by the Air Ministry.

K7208 was one of the initial production batch of 34 MkIs which were completed in 1937. This aircraft was sent to the Aircraft and Armament Experimental Establishment where it was converted into a MkIV prototype being fitted with Rolls-Royce Merlin IV engines. In total some forty MkIV Whitleys were built; some were equipped with Merlin X engines.

In the early years of the Second World War Bomber Command relied heavily on three bomber types, the Vickers Wellington, the Handley Page Hampden and the Whitley. It was Whitleys which carried out the first night raid of the war on the 3rd-4th September when two Squadrons, Nos. 51 and 58 from Leconfield, dropped leaflets over Germany.

HAWKER HECTOR
A beautiful study in light and shade of a Hawker Hector. Powered by a Napier Dagger engine, the Hector was used for army co-operation work. The hook, which was lowered for message collection, can be seen between the undercarriage legs. K8090 was built by Westlands and delivered to the Aircraft & Armament Experimental Establishment and the Royal Aircraft Establishment for appraisal. It was finally struck off charge in February 1942. The Hector was the last development of the line of Hawker Hart variants.

HANDLEY PAGE HARROW

A delightful study of K6933, the first production Handley Page Harrow which flew in May 1935.

The Harrow was issued to Bomber Command in 1937 and although the type was quickly replaced by Wellingtons it did provide valuable experience of monoplane handling techniques.

The Harrow, powered by two Bristol Pegasus XX engines, was capable of 200 mph with a bomb load of some 3,000 lb.

When war broke out in 1939 the type was used in the role it had originally been designed for, as a transport aircraft. Some continued in use until late in 1944.

FAIREY SWORDFISH I
A Fairey Swordfish I of No. 810 Squadron in flight over *HMS Ark Royal* during exercises in 1939.

ARMSTRONG WHITWORTH ENSIGN
Newly introduced into service the prestigious Armstrong Whitworth Ensign was a most impressive addition to the Imperial Airways fleet. This photograph of the Ensign demonstrates the sheer size of the new aeroplane.

SUPERMARINE WALRUS

The Supermarine Seagull V first flew on 21st June 1933 and was conceived as a private venture amphibian reconnaissance aircraft capable of being catapulted from warships.
After successful trials with the RAF the Air Ministry placed orders for the type, known as the Walrus.
Production in the UK of the Walrus ceased in 1944 after some 741 aircraft had been produced by Supermarine and Saros. Used extensively for Air Sea Rescue work the Walrus earned tremendous respect during the Second World War.

VICKERS WELLESLEY
Vickers Wellesleys of No. 14 Squadron fly over the Jordan Hills, Palestine, in the spring of 1939. Initial delivery of the type to No. 14 Squadron began in August 1938 and they would remain in service until December 1940.
On 11th June 1940 the Squadron attacked Massana airfield and successfully destroyed aircraft and hangars and set fire to 35,000 gallons of petrol.
The Wellesley was replaced in No. 14 Squadron by Blenheim's in 1941.

WESTLAND LYSANDER *(opposite)*
The Westland Lysander was designed as an Army Co-operation aircraft with a STOL capability. It was immensely strong making it ideal for use as a Special Duties aircraft, being able to land on unprepared fields and small airstrips.
A total of 1,368 Lysanders were constructed by Westland at Yeovil. All were powered by Bristol Mercury variants which gave ample power to enable the Lysander to be successfully used as a target and glider tug.

L4717

VICKERS WELLINGTON

One of the great aircraft of the Second World War, the Vickers Wellington. The design was commenced in 1932 and the prototype first flew in 1936, immediate production orders followed as the expanding RAF realised its potential as a heavy bomber.

The construction of the Wellington was of particular interest, taking a construction method of Dr Barnes Wallis called Geodetic, in effect a metal exoskeleton with fabric covering, light, strong and not easily affected by battle damage.

Powered by Bristol Pegasus radial engines the Wellington I was capable of carrying a 4,500 lb bomb load and a crew of 5.

This magnificent study of No. 9 Squadron Wellington I's in formation was taken en-route to or from the Brussels Aero Exhibition held in 1939. The Squadron, and probably these aircraft, took part in the second RAF bombing raid of the war when they attacked German shipping at Brunsbüttel on the 4th September 1939.

1939-45

On September 3rd, 1939 war was declared between Great Britain and Nazi Germany. This great conflict would last for five years and would cost many millions of lives. It would be a period of intense activity with great advances in technology.

In the air, the feeble giants of a Bomber Command formed in 1936 would become strong and finally capable of delivering the atom bomb, a weapon that would shake whole nations in one attack.

Charles Brown was, at the time of Mr. Chamberlain's announcement of the declaration of war, operating from his Fleet Street business in Shoe Lane. He continued with press work throughout the Battle of France and the Battle of Britain, taking aeronautical commissions along the way. He lived with his wife and daughter in Worcester Park and was involved as an ARP warden in local affairs. Press assignments for the magazine *Aeronautics* ensured that Charles Brown, accompanied by his faithful Alsatian *Ronto,* would spend most of his time on aviation topics.

Late in 1941 Charles Brown was commissioned by the magazine *Flying* to take colour photographs of aviation subjects. The colour stock was rare, but this transatlantic deal ensured that there exists an unsurpassed colour record of aircraft in the Second World War.

From bases in the UK to assignment with the 2nd Tactical Air Force in the low countries Charles Brown was able to maintain his very high standard of aviation photography and despite operational pressures, he was able to portray war planes with his particular skill. A small portion of this magnificent record is reproduced in this section.

BLACKBURN BOTHA

The Blackburn Botha, was designed for Coastal Command for general reconnaissance or torpedo-bomber duties. Powered by two Bristol Pegasus engines the Botha was considered underpowered, this and other shortcomings led to its only being sent to two squadrons, Nos. 608 and 502. Bothas patrolled the North Sea until they were withdrawn operationally in April 1941, only twenty months after entering service. Many were subsequently used in Air Navigation and Air Gunnery Schools until 1944.

SUPERMARINE WALRUS
A beautiful silhouette of a Supermarine Walrus.

WELLINGTON II

Merlin powered Wellington II, W5461 makes a fine study as it formates with the camera aircraft. This aircraft was lost on a night raid to Berlin on the 12/13th of August 1941.

HANDLEY PAGE HAMPDEN I *(opposite)*

A Handley Page Hampden I, AT137 of No. 455 Squadron photographed in 1942. The Hampden was a twin engined heavy bomber ordered into service in 1938. By 1942 the type had been superseded in many squadrons by more advanced aircraft like the Stirling, Halifax and Lancaster. However the Hampden continued in use as a torpedo-bomber with Coastal Command.

No. 455 Squadron, formed in June 1941 as a bomber squadron, was transferred to Coastal Command in April 1942. This photograph was probably taken when the exchange had taken place.

T UB

SHORT STIRLING I
War-weary Short Stirling Is in formation over East Anglia. These aeroplanes from No. 1651 Heavy Conversion Unit were based at Waterbeach. This fine picture was taken on 29th April 1942.

WESTLAND WHIRLWIND I

A Westland Whirlwind I on a test flight. This aeroplane served with No. 137 Squadron, initially based at Charmy Down in November 1941.
This Whirlwind subsequently carried the civil registration G-AGOI.

SUPERMARINE SPITFIRE XI
Photo Reconnaissance Supermarine Spitfire XI, EN654 flying over a wintery English landscape. The photograph was taken in November 1943.

ARMSTRONG WHITWORTH WHITLEY V
Armstrong Whitworth Whitley Vs of No. 78 Squadron of the Yorkshire based 4 Group, Bomber Command. The squadron operated Whitleys from 1937 until March 1942 when the last of their Merlin powered Mk.Vs were replaced by Handley Page Halifaxes. Whitleys from No. 78 Squadron took part in some of the earliest raids of the war against Germany.
This photograph captures the nose down attitude adopted by the aeroplane in level flight.

VICKERS WELLINGTONS Mk.IIs

Vickers Wellingtons of No. 104 Squadron pose for the camera somewhere near their base at Driffield in Yorkshire in April 1941. The aircraft are Wellington Mk.IIs and are easily distinguishable from the earlier mark of Wellington by being fitted with Rolls-Royce Merlin X engines which improved the types load-carrying capacity, its operating altitude and cruising speed.

The Squadron continued to use the Wellington until 1945 when it became re-equipped with Consolidated B.VI Liberators.

HANDLEY PAGE HALIFAX
In November 1940 No. 35 Squadron was reformed to operate the new Handley Page Halifax and establish its use for night operations. The squadron was selected, in August 1942, as one of the first five squadrons to form the Pathfinder Force.
The Halifax was replaced by the Avro Lancaster in No. 35 Squadron in March 1944, however this classic study of a Halifax BII Series I was taken in the type's heyday with the Squadron.

FORTRESS Mk.I
In May 1941 No. 90 Squadron of the RAF was selected to receive and operate B-17, Fortress Mk.I aeroplanes. Thus equipped the squadron carried out high altitude daylight bombing raids against targets in Europe. Operating from Polebrook they flew operationally until February 1942. The indifferent results, experienced during 51 daylight raids, did nothing to dissuade Bomber Command from its night bombing policies.
This superb photograph is of a No. 90 Squadron Fortress I, AN530, code letters F-WP.

HAWKER HURRICANE IIc

A Hawker Hurricane IIc night fighter issued to No. 87 Squadron RAF. This squadron fought in France and the Battle of Britain ending up, in September 1940, in the west country concentrating on night intruder attacks on the French mainland.

Hawker Hurricane IIcs with cannon armament and Merlin XX engines began to re-equip the Squadron in June 1941 at which time it operated at Colerne and St. Marys on the Scillies.

MILES M.25 MARTINET

A Miles M.25 Martinet was basically a Master trainer modified especially for target towing duties. To accommodate the heavy winch and towing gear, the engine a Bristol Mercury XX or XXX radial was moved further forward and many other redesign details were necessary.

The prototype first flew in 1942 and many hundreds of Martinets were shortly in service.

Martinets were to prove invaluable in Air Gunnery, Operational Training Units and Anti-Aircraft Co-operation Squadrons between 1943 and their final replacement by Tempest target tugs after the war. Some 1,724 were finally built.

SHORT STIRLING Is
Short Stirling Is of No. 1651 Heavy Conversion Unit based at Waterbeach in April 1942.
The Short Stirling was the first multi-engined bomber to enter RAF service, being introduced into operational use by No. 7 Squadron based at Oakington in the latter part of 1940.

WESTLAND WHIRLWIND

The Westland Whirlwind fighter took a lot of development before it was a smooth functioning weapon. The first squadron to receive the type was No. 263, based initially at Grangemouth in July 1940. Whirlwinds continued in useful service with the squadron until December 1943.

This interesting photograph of pilots of No. 263 Squadron was taken at Warmwell in the autumn of 1942.

During the course of the Second World War only two squadrons were equipped with the Whirlwind, the second was No. 137.

HAWKER SEA HURRICANE
A Hawker Sea Hurricane IB in formation with two Supermarine Seafire IIC's of No. 760 Squadron based at Yeovilton. This fine study was taken on the 18th November 1942.

MUSTANG I
This study of a North American Mustang I was taken on 24th July 1942. In its early form the Mustang was used principally for photo-reconnaissance. This Mustang is from No. 2 Squadron based at Sawbridgeworth.

SUPERMARINE SPITFIRE V *(opposite)*
One in a series of studies made by Charles Brown of Spitfire V, R6923, an early example of the type in service with No. 97 Squadron.
Early production aircraft were delivered to 97 Squadron then based at Biggin Hill, in February 1941.

FAIREY ALBACORE

Fairey Albacore was designed as a replacement for the Swordfish; in fact the Albacore never took over from the Swordfish but merely supplemented it as a Torpedo Strike and Reconnaissance aircraft. Following successful trials, production of the Albacore began in 1939 and some 800 were produced by 1943 when production ceased.

In its heyday in mid 1942, 15 Squadrons used the type. They were engaged in a wide range of activities; on Russian convoy patrols, in the Mediterranean on anti-shipping strikes, anti-submarine patrols and in the Indian Ocean on similar duties. The Albacore was also used in the Western Desert dropping flares as an information back-up to the Battle of El Alamein. By 1944 the Albacore had been phased out of service with the Fleet Air Arm.

FAIREY BARRACUDA
In January 1939 the Air Ministry placed a contract for two prototypes of a new torpedo/dive bomber designed by Fairey. An odd looking aeroplane with its shoulder wing and Fairey-Youngman flaps, which acted as dive brakes, it was designated Type 100 and later called the Barracuda. After many development crises the first production aircraft flew in May 1942. The Mk.I & IIs were three seater carrierborne or shore based aircraft of all metal construction, the Mk.I was powered by a 1,260 hp Rolls-Royce Merlin 30 and the Mk.II by a 1,680 hp Merlin 32.
The Barracuda first entered service in January 1943 and finally ceased first-line service in 1953.

GRUMMAN HELLCATS
Grumman Hellcats of the Fleet Air Arm began to arrive from America under lend-lease arrangements in 1943. A total of 1,182 Hellcats were supplied to the Navy. The first unit to receive Hellcats was No. 800 Squadron which used the type successfully on anti-shipping strikes off the Norwegian coast. The Squadron was based on board *HMS Ocean.* The type was involved in many actions in home waters and in South East Asia. One of the last Hellcats in the Royal Navy was in use at Lossiemouth as late as April 1953.

HAWKER HURRICANE Mk. IV *(opposite)*
Charles Brown took a series of beautiful studies of the prototype Hurricane Mk. IV. The aeroplane is equipped with tropical filters and carries 2 x 40mm Vickers 'S' cannons which were intended to destroy tanks. The type was used in Italy and the Balkans. The photograph was probably taken in 1943.

KZ193

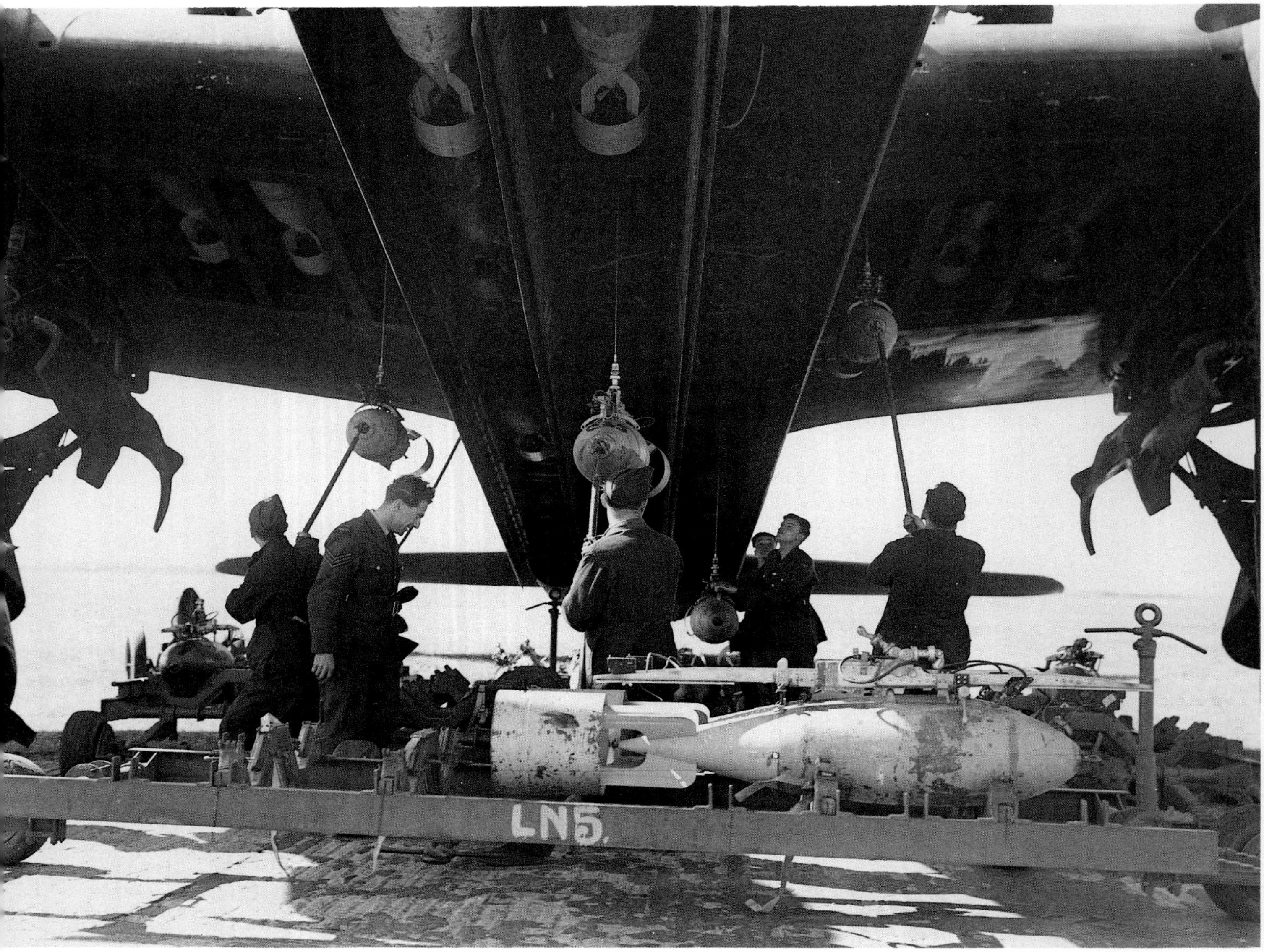

SHORT STIRLING
Bombing up a Short Stirling at No. 1651 Heavy Conversion Unit at Waterbeach, April 1942.

CHANCE VOUGHT CORSAIR

The first Squadron to be equipped with the Chance Vought Corsair was No. 1830, who received Lend-Lease aircraft in June 1943. The Squadron trained in Quoncet and then shipped aboard *HMS Illustrious.*

The formation photograph is of Corsair IIs of No. 1830 Squadron.

SHORT STIRLING CREW
A well known but none the less evocative photograph of a Short Stirling crew being briefed for a formation detail. The unit is No. 1651 Heavy Conversion Unit flying operationally retired aircraft. This photograph was taken in April 1942.

HAWKER TYPHOON
Some 34 squadrons of the RAF were to receive the ferocious Hawker Typhoon which would become one of the principle fighter bombers used in the allied advance through France and Holland in 1944.
Powered by the temperamental Napier Sabre II 24-cylinder sleeve valve engine which developed 2,180 hp, the Typhoon was in July 1941 when the type first entered service, the fastest fighter of the war with a top speed of 405 mph at 18,000 feet.
This magnificent photograph shows an early production Mk.IB Typhoon.

HALIFAX B2
There has scarcely been such a perfect backdrop to any aeroplane picture, as the skyscape captured behind this Halifax II of No. 35 Squadron. The squadron received its first Halifax in November 1940 and operated the type until 1944.

MILES MARTINET
A fine study of a Target Towing Miles Martinet, HN862 which was one of the aircraft built by Phillips and Powis at Woodley. In all a total of 1,724 Martinet aircraft were produced between 1942 and 1945.
This photograph was probably taken for the company and before the aircraft had been allocated to a unit.

4F
4M

SUPERMARINE SPITFIRE VB
Supermarine Spitfire VB, BL479 of No. 316 (City of Warsaw) Squadron photographed on the 6th August 1943. At this time the squadron was operating from Northolt.

GRUMMAN AVENGER *(opposite)*
Nearly 10,000 Grumman Avengers were built and the type was used extensively in the US Navy and the Fleet Air Arm. This type, featuring a power operated gun turret and capable of carrying a 22 inch torpedo, equipped 15 squadrons of the Fleet Air Arm.
These Avengers are from No. 846 Squadron and were photographed in December 1943.

REPUBLIC P-47C THUNDERBOLT
A 'little friend', a Republic P-47C, Thunderbolt long range escort fighter poses briefly in front of a Boeing B-17E.
The Thunderbolt was an extremely strong fighter and was much liked by its pilots. Together with the P-38 Lightning and the P-51 Mustang, these fighters escorted the USAAF's heavy bombers to and from their targets, deep in occupied Europe.
This aircraft was from the 56th Fighter Group.

DE HAVILLAND MOSQUITO VI

In October 1944 No. 143 Squadron was equipped with de Havilland Mosquito VI aircraft. The Squadron was based at Banff and flew its aircraft on RP-equipped (Rocket Projectile) recces along the Norwegian coast. The Squadron's last strike was carried out on 3rd May 1945 against installations at Kiel. On 25th May the Squadron was disbanded.

This interesting photograph of a No. 143 Squadron Mosquito was taken by Charles Brown in February 1945.

AVRO LANCASTER BI PP687

Posed for the camera and showing all the details and textures that suggest a new aeroplane on a factory test flight, PP687 was built by Vickers Armstrong at Castle Bromwich in 1945 and was supplied to No. 149 Squadron in March of that year. It was subsequently struck off charge in December 1946. Born on the production line of the less successful Avro Manchester the Lancaster was perhaps the most famous and versatile heavy bomber of World War II. Many photographs exist of the type but Charles E. Brown managed to capture, in a few photographs of the Lancaster, some beautiful images.

LANCASTER BII

An unidentified Lancaster BII, one of 300 built by Armstrong Whitworth at Baginton. The principle difference with the BII was the fitting of 1,735 hp Bristol Hercules radial engines in place of the Rolls-Royce Merlin for the Mk.I and III.

FAIREY BARRACUDA
Barracudas of the Fleet Air Arm set out for an anti-shipping strike.

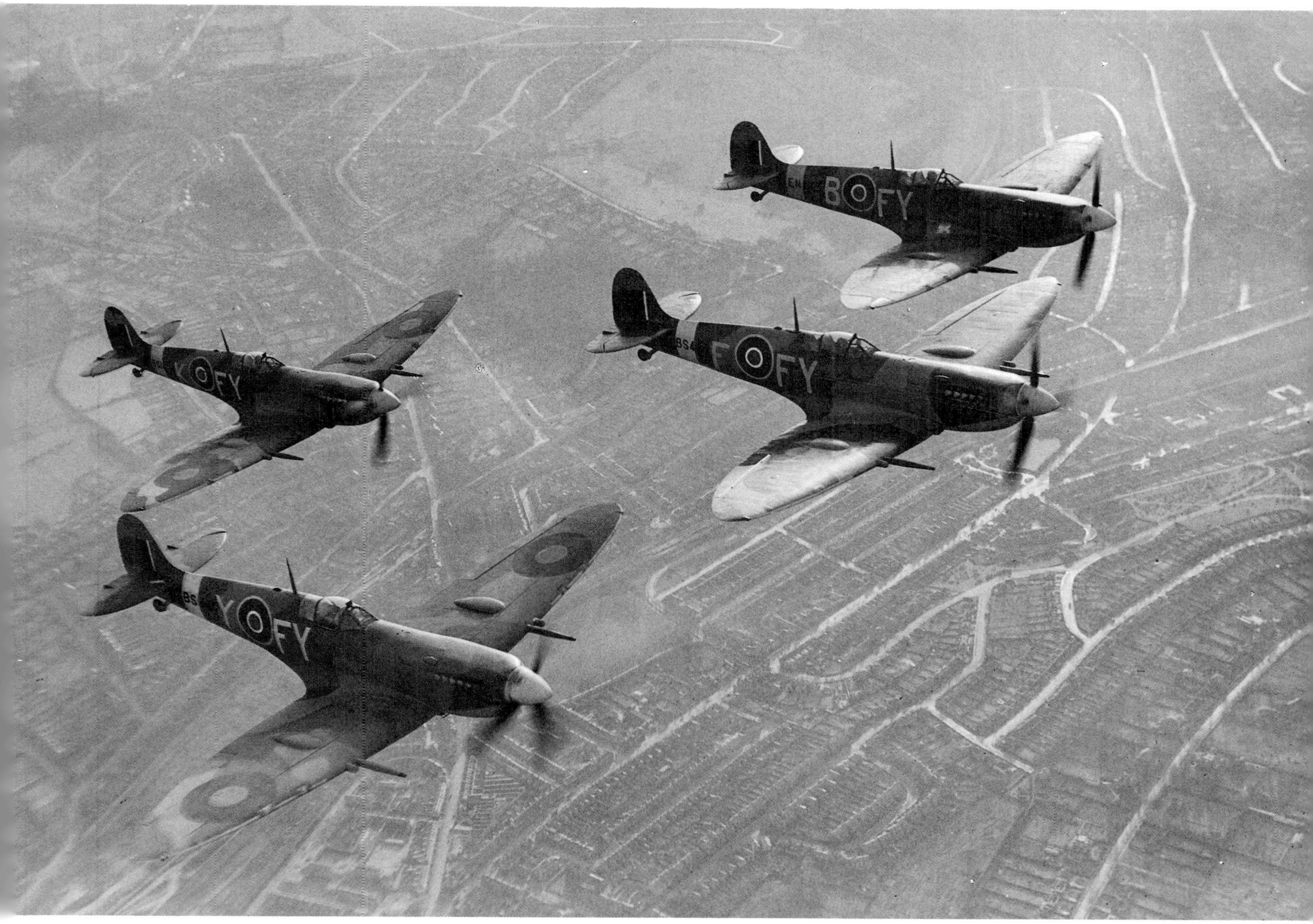

SUPERMARINE SPITFIRE Mk.IX
Supermarine Spitfire Mk.IXs of No. 611 Squadron, which was one of the first units to operate that particular mark of Spitfire, receiving their aircraft in July 1942.

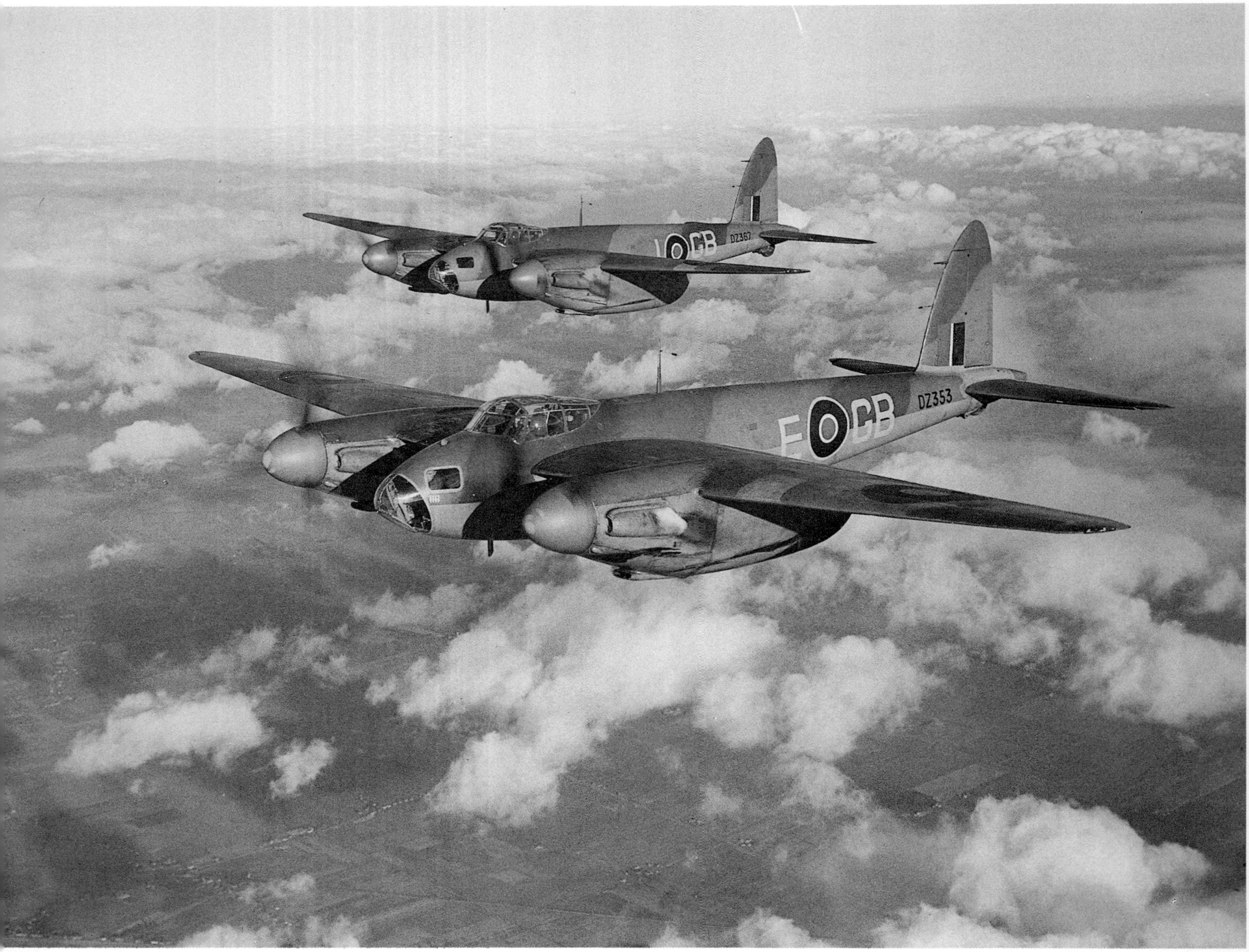

DE HAVILLAND MOSQUITO
The first RAF Squadron to receive the superlative de Havilland Mosquito was No. 105 Squadron. It was this Squadron, on 26th September 1942 which made the low level daylight attack on the Gestapo Headquarters in Oslo. Following this heroic exploit the press turned its attention to the Mosquito and No. 105 Squadron. These two aircraft are from No. 105 Squadron and were photographed in December 1942 when the Squadron was based at Marham in Norfolk.

MOSQUITO B.XVI
A Mosquito B.XVI of No. 571 Squadron.

B-26C MARAUDER II
The B-26C Marauder II was used extensively by the US Army Ninth Air Force squadrons, based in the UK. Heavily armed with 11 x .50 calibre machine guns, the Marauder could carry 2,460 lb of bombs at 274 mph. Its relatively high landing speed and the long take-off run tended to restrict the number of airfields the type could utilize.
In June 1944 production of the Marauder ceased after a total of 1,585 aircraft had been completed.
This photograph was taken after 'D'-Day and was operating in support of the Allied invasion of occupied Europe.

AVRO LANCASTER BI *(opposite)*
A beautiful head-on portrait of an Avro Lancaster BI on a test flight in 1944.

SERVICING CREWS
As vital as aircrew to the success of Bomber Command were the tireless efforts of servicing crews.
Here fitters work high up on the Rolls-Royce Merlin engines of an Avro Lancaster.

MOSQUITO Mk.16
A mood photograph of a Photo Reconnaissance Mosquito Mk.16, NS777 of No. 140 Squadron. The squadron was part of the 2nd Tactical Air Force and moved, in support of the allied advance, into France in September 1944. This photograph was taken sometime during the winter of 1944/45 when the Squadron was based at Melsbroek.

HAWKER TEMPEST V

Hawker Tempest V NV696 being flown on test from the production assembly plant at Langley on 29th November 1944. The pilot could be Bill Humble who had flown several photographic sorties for Charles Brown.

BOEING B-17G
A lovely study of a Boeing B-17G of the 709th Bomber Squadron of the 447th Bomber Group, United States Army Air Force. This photograph was probably taken just after the war in Europe came to an end in May 1945.

SHORT SHETLAND
The Short Shetland in flight in May 1945. Sadly the aeroplane, which had superb handling qualities, never developed past the prototype stage.

SUPERMARINE SPITFIRE Mk.XII
Supermarine Spitfire Mk.XII poses for this magnificent study. The Mk.XII was the first operational version of the Spitfire to be fitted with a Rolls-Royce Griffon engine and was designated type 366. The aircraft had a maximum speed of 393 mph at 18,000 feet and a ceiling of 40,000 feet.
The Mk.XII was initially issued to Nos. 41 and 91 based at Hawkinge in the spring of 1943. MB882 was the last Mk.XII and was operated by No. 41 Squadron.

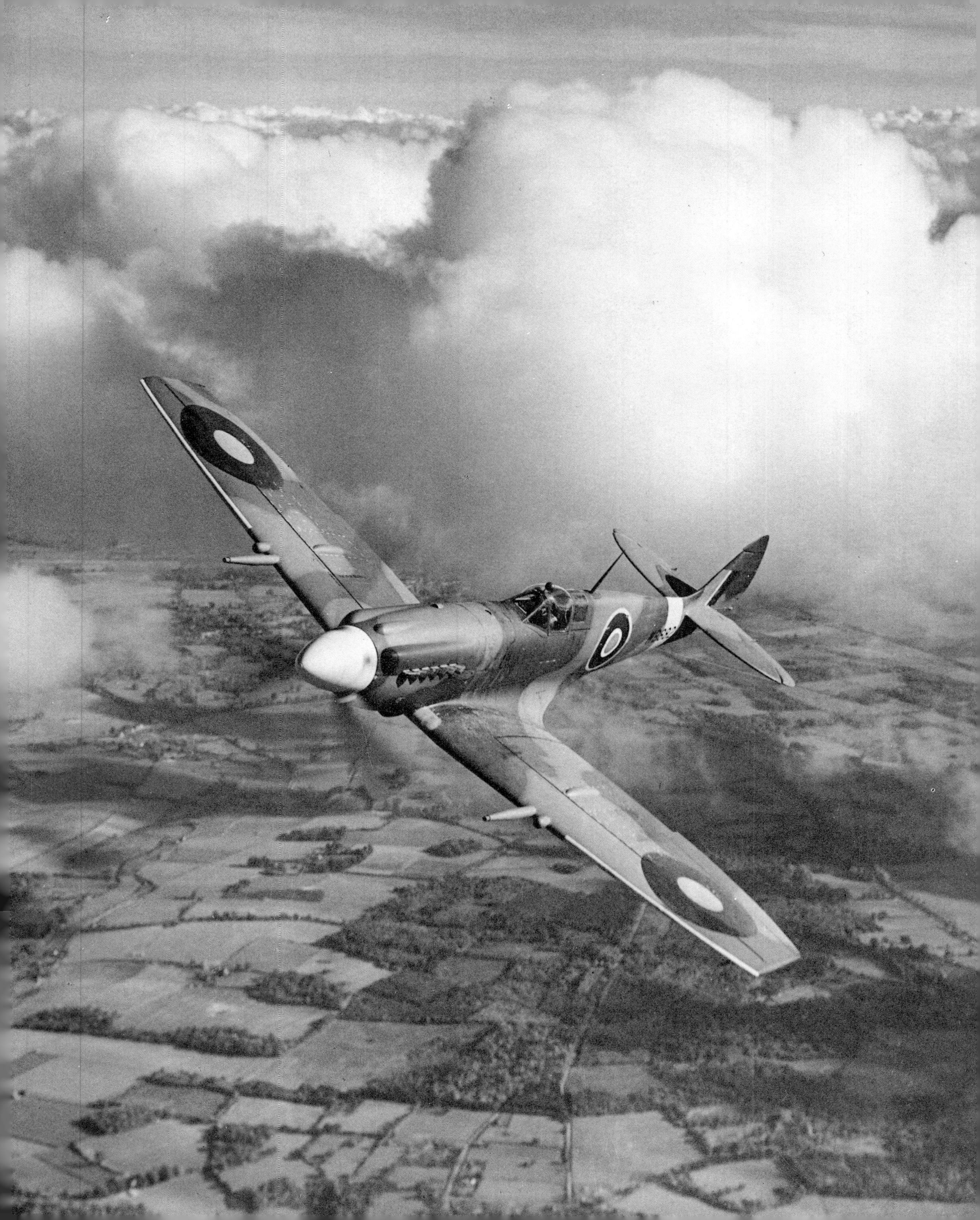

HAWKER TEMPEST V
A beautiful formation photograph of Hawker Tempest Vs of No. 501 Squadron. In August 1944 this squadron was busy converting on to the Tempest V and by the 11 August the squadron became operational by day and night flying to intercept V1 flying bombs. The patrols flown were known as anti-"diver" and the squadron continued with this work until the end of the war.
During the period of its anti-"diver" work the squadron was based at Manston, Bradwell Bay and Hansdon.

FAIREY FIREFLY FI *(opposite)*
A Fairey Firefly FI on test. This early production aircraft was one of 132 Mk.Is produced at Hanworth, delivery began in December 1943. Four 20mm cannons and the new 1,730 hp Rolls-Royce Griffon IIB engine made the Firefly a tremendous advance over the Fulman. They were used extensively by the Fleet Air Arm as fighters.

HAWKER TEMPEST V
Two Hawker Tempest V's both powered by the 24-cylinder Napier Sabre engine. The aircraft in the foreground is fitted with an experimental annualar radiator whilst the other aeroplane appears to be standard in every way.

SHORT SHETLAND
The first prototype of the Short Shetland flew in the early part of 1945. The huge all metal flying boat was powered by four Bristol Centaurus engines and could achieve 267 mph at 4,000 feet. The Shetland was designated Type S.35 and was originally, in 1940, intended to replace the Sunderland as an anti-submarine patrol and reconnaissance aircraft.

AVRO YORK

The growing need for transport aircraft led to the development, in only five months, of the Avro York, the first of which flew from Manchester Ringway in 1942.

This rapid development was due in no small part to the use of Lancaster components wherever possible.

G-AGJC was given the serial number MW113 and was delivered to BOAC in July 1944. It is photographed in its wartime livery, dark earth and dark green camouflage with the red, white and blue fuselage flashes adopted by civil airliners at that period.

1945 onwards

Aviation progress since the Second World War has been greater than at any other time. The impetus of technology generated by the war could not be checked even though the armed services diminished in size over the ensuing years of peace

Charles Brown was recognised as a leader in the field of aviation photography and in this exciting era of development and experiment, his skills were eagerly sought by manufacturers who wished for first class images of their latest products.

The combination of jet-age technology and his consummate experience and skill using his faithful few cameras, led to the creation of his finest work. He captured on film, images of the first Meteor jet fighters in the RAF and continued photographing all the major types of aircraft produced. That is until his failing health and the more stringent physical limits put upon aircrew, combined to put a stop to his flying career.

One of the last assignments he carried out involved the Hawker P1127, predecessor of the now famous Harrier.

In his great days it was said by other journalists that if Charles Brown had completed an assignment, then they might as well not bother. He would spend many hours looking for just the right moment for his photographs whilst many of his peers would only take a few minutes flying time. The results are telling and it is hardly surprising that he should have been honoured by various societies for his outstanding work.

That such a brilliant photographic record of prototype and early development aircraft exists is a testament to the esteem in which the aviation world held Charles Brown and his work during the jet-age.

VICKERS ARMSTRONG SPITEFUL XIV
The Vickers Armstrong Spiteful XIV was a direct descendant of the Spitfire and was designed in 1944.
With a Rolls-Royce Griffon 65 or 69 engine the Spiteful was capable of some 470 mph in level flight.
Few of this ultimate Spitfire development were built and the type did not enter Squadron service.

GLOSTER METEOR Mk.IV
A beautiful study of a Gloster Meteor Mk.IV. *(opposite)*

HAWKER TEMPEST V
A Hawker Tempest V cruises across the Wiltshire countryside having just taken part in smoke laying experiments. The smoke generators are mounted below the wings.

SEA MOSQUITO
The Admiralty issued a Specification No. 15/44 for a twin-engined aircraft capable of carrier operations.
The Mosquito was suitably developed leading to the successful carrier landings in March 1944.
Production Sea Mosquitos became known as TR Mk.33s and a total of fifty were produced.
Mosquito TW256 is a TR 33 flying from Lee-on-Solent.

SUPERMARINE SEA OTTER
Every detail is clearly visible in this photograph of a Supermarine Sea Otter. This type entered service with the Fleet Air Arm in 1944 and was successfully used until helicopters became available for rescue and communication work in the early 1950s.

A total of 290 Sea Otters were produced between 1943 and 1946, the aircraft was similar to but more efficient than the Walrus which it replaced. Four Squadrons were equipped with Sea Otters whilst other units as far as apart as Lee-on-Solent and Hong Kong also used the type.

GLOSTER METEOR Mk.4

A clear sunny day on the south coast; a delightful setting in which to photograph an immaculate Meteor Mk.4. The balloons suggest that this photograph was taken in connection with the World Air Speed Record attempt.

EE528 was known to have been used by the RAE at Farnborough and NGTE between 1951 and 1955, where many tests were carried out on engines and controls.

GLOSTER METEOR F.4

In an attempt to increase the sales of their aircraft, the Gloster Company in 1947 took a Meteor F.4 from the production line. It was modified with extra fuel tankage and the armament removed. Registered G-AIDC, it was successfully demonstrated in European countries until it was crashed by a Belgian Air Force pilot.

The remains were bought back to England and were to form the basis of a T.7 demonstrator which would also be used for touring. The aeroplane was re-registered G-AKPK and began its demonstration tour on 20th May 1948.

In one month the Meteor flew 5,000 miles, made 61 take-offs and landings and carried 31 passengers of five nationalities. The photograph is of G-AKPK in red and white ready for its sales tour.

LANCASTER BIs
During the summer of 1946 the RAF made a goodwill tour of the United States and the Squadron chosen to represent the service was No. 35. In this impressive photograph, the Squadron's Lancaster BI's form into echelon starboard for the camera. All the aircraft are painted in the post-war colour scheme of black and white.
All the Squadron's Lancasters were replaced in 1949 by Avro Lincolns.
At the time of their despatch to America the Squadron was based at Graveley where it had been since 1942.

DE HAVILLAND HORNET
The delicate de Havilland Hornet made its first flight on 28th July 1944. Made of wood in the same style as the Mosquito, the Hornet was incredibly light and possessed enormous performance potential with over 4,000 hp available from its two Rolls-Royce Merlin engines.
PX217 is a Hornet F. Mk.I being flown by Pat Fillingham, one of the de Havilland production test pilots.

TEMPEST II
Designed for operations against the Japanese in the Far East, the Tempest II differed from the already successful and mass produced Tempest V in having the newly developed Bristol Centaurus sleeve valve radial engine fitted, which gave the aircraft a speed of 440 mph at 15,000 feet.
A total of 450 aircraft were constructed, the first entering service with No. 54 Fighter Squadron at Chilbolton.

BLACKBURN FIREBRAND TF5

A Blackburn Firebrand TF5 of the Fleet Air Arm. Conceived in 1939 the Firebrand did not get into squadron service until 1945 when it was finally developed into a torpedo-carrying strike fighter. A total of 220 Firebrands were constructed including Mk.V & Va. The type was superseded in service by the Westland Wyvern in 1953.

The Firebrand was powered by a Bristol Centaurus XI engine and could achieve a maximum speed of 340 mph.

HAWKER SEA FURY
The last piston engined fighter to be operated by the Fleet Air Arm was the Hawker Sea Fury. Capable of 460 mph at 18,000 feet the Sea Fury was a formidable aircraft when it entered service in 1947, being superseded by the jet powered Sea Hawks, in Fleet Air Arm front line service, by 1953.
TF947 is a Sea Fury produced between 1946 and 1952 and is a Mk.F10 powered by a Bristol Centaurus 18 radial engine capable of 2,480 hp.

MILES MESSENGER M.38

Flying over the Berkshire countryside near Woodley, this Miles M.38 Messenger in its blue and black post-war livery, makes a delightful study.

The M.38 Messenger first flew in September 1942 as a development of the M.28. It differed in having a fixed undercarriage which made for simplicity. The Messenger as its name implies was built, in small numbers, for the RAF who used it for communication work. The Messenger was powered by a Gipsy Major engine and was capable of a top speed of 115 mph.

FAIREY FIREFLY

In March 1944 further developments were carried out on the Fairey Firefly to bring the aircraft up to Mk.4 standard.

In total 160 Mk.4s were built, the first actually flying in May 1946. Amongst the more noticeable changes in basic shape are the clipped wing tips, increased fin area and outer wing nacelles carrying ASH radar and fuel.

AVRO LINCOLN
Derived from the Avro Lancaster and in fact originally referred to as the Lancaster IV, the Avro Lincoln was to appear too late to play an active part in the Second World War.
Powered with Rolls-Royce Merlin 83 engines the Lincoln could achieve a top speed of 310 mph at 18,300 feet.
The first squadron to take delivery of the type was No. 57 based at East Kirkby initially with only three aircraft, one of which was RF385.

HAWKER FBXI SEA FURY
A Hawker FBXI Sea Fury of the Fleet Air Arm.

AVRO TUDOR MK.IV

Star Leopard was an Avro Tudor Mk.IV of British South American Airways. These early post-war airliners, of which four were sold to BSAA, were put into service on the South Atlantic routes in October 1947.

The Tudor was able to carry 32 passengers. In 1950, after being used as freighters in the Berlin airlift, the Tudors of BSAA were delivered to Hurn and Ringway for storage. They never flew again.

VAMPIRE F3

The de Havilland Vampire F3 entered RAF service in 1947 and was used as a single seater jet fighter. By the 1950's many had become obsolete and the FB5 variants had taken their place in fighter squadrons.

The F3 had still much strategical value and sold readily to a number of air forces. This photograph, one of Charles Brown's best, is of a Norwegian Air Force Vampire F3 of No. 332 Squadron. It was photographed in June 1949.

ARMSTRONG WHITWORTH METEOR NF14
The NF14 was the final version of the Meteor night fighter, being issued to the RAF between October 1953 and May 1954. Photographed in detail in this beautiful study are NF14s from No. 152 Squadron.

FAIREY FIREFLY T.1

Fairey Firefly T.1 trainers photographed early in 1948. The Royal Naval trainer in the background 22027, was converted from an early Mk.1 fighter.
The T.1 in the foreground is destined for the Royal Netherlands Naval Air Service.
A total of 34 T.1 trainers were built.

HAWKER HUNTER F2 *(opposite)*
Hawker Hunter F2s of No. 257 Squadron, photographed in November 1954.

GLOSTER METEOR F4
Gloster Meteor F4, EE521. In 1948 the Meteor Mk.III had been superseded by the F.4 which had up-rated Derwent 5 engines. The F.4 delivered was V2436 in April 1950, by which time 24 RAF squadrons were using the type.

WN950
WN950

SARO SR A/1
Photographed on 29th July 1947 was the unusual Saro SR A/1. This jet powered fighter with a flying boat hull was a revolutionary concept. Sadly the experiment came to naught but TG263 still exists and is kept at the Imperial War Musueum at Duxford.

HAWKER HUNTER F2
The first RAF Squadron to receive Hawker Hunter F2 fighters was No. 257, based at Wattisham and which received the aircraft as replacements for Meteor F8s in November 1954.
This photograph captures the Squadron's pilots grouped before the aircraft on the hardstand at Wattisham. The yellow and green chequers, the Squadron's insignia, were painted on the nose shortly after.

ENGLISH ELECTRIC CANBERRA *(opposite)*
The first jet bomber to serve with the RAF was the English Electric Canberra, the prototype of which first flew on 13th May 1949. Following the successful trials the fifth prototype was designated B2.
Posing for some superb formation photographs are Canberra B2s of Nos. 61 and 109 Squadrons. The B2s were first introduced into service in May 1951.

HANDLEY PAGE HASTINGS
A fine study of the Handley Page Hastings C2s of No. 70 Squadron which acquired the type in 1956 when the Squadron was based in Cyprus. The Squadron continued to use the type until 1968.
No. 70 Squadron aircraft had the white "LXX" numerals painted on a black diamond displayed on the fin. This was removed when the Squadron returned to the UK in 1975.
The Hastings, a long range transport aircraft, was powered by four Bristol Hercules 106 engines and could carry a load in the region of 32,000 lbs including fuel with a 1,690 miles range in normal circumstances. Introduced into No. 47 Squadron in 1948 the type played its part in the Berlin Airlift which ended in 1949. Besides operating the Command's main passenger routes to the Middle and Far East the Hastings was used by the airborne forces as paratroop and supply-droppers.

HUNTING PERCIVAL JET PROVOST
In order to create a more direct route to pilot handling of service jet aircraft, RAF Flying Training Command adopted the Hunting Percival Jet Provost in 1953. The Jet Provost is still a valued training aeroplane in the RAF and many other air forces. Powered with an Armstrong Siddeley Viper 101 jet engine, the two seater trainer was capable of 330 mph at 20,000 feet.
XM370 was one of the first production aircraft.

WESTLAND WYVERN *(opposite)*
The first Squadron in the Fleet Air Arm to receive the torpedo carrying strike aircraft, the Westland Wyvern, was No. 813.
The Wyvern was the first turbo-prop to enter squadron service and was in its brief career capable of carrying bombs, depth charges, mines or rockets in addition to its four 20mm cannon armament. This serene photograph was taken by Charles Brown before an inspection at Ford by the Duke of Edinburgh in October 1953.

182
188
187
192
183
184

VICKERS VALIANT
The Vickers Valiant was designed for Bomber Command and was intended to be able to carry any type of bomb including the 'Nuclear deterrent' at high altitude and at speeds around Mach 0.9. An Air Ministry specification was issued in 1948 to progress the Vickers 660 high performance bomber. In 1949 a contract was placed for a prototype powered by four Rolls-Royce Avon engines and on the 18th May 1952 the first Valiant flew.
The subject of this superb portrait is WB215, the second Valiant which first flew on 11th April 1952. The type was successfully introduced into the RAF in 1954 when No. 232 Operational Conversion Unit was formed at Gaydon to train V-force Squadrons in the operation of Valiants, the first V bombers.

FOLLAND MIDGE *(opposite)*
The prototype Folland Midge in its beautiful blue and red paint scheme poses below the rear doors of a Fairchild 119C prior to the SBAC show at Farnborough.
The little fighter did not see RAF service but it was to lead to the development of the Gnat which became an important training aid within the service.

HANDLEY PAGE VICTOR
In 1954 crowds at Farnborough saw for the first time the huge 'crescent' winged V bomber, the HP Victor.

FAIREY DELTA FD2

The Fairey Delta FD2 gained the World Air Speed Record by achieving an average speed of 1,132 mph on 10th March 1956. The little aeroplane was piloted by Peter Twiss who had to fly with extreme accuracy during the 31 seconds it took to fly the 15 kilometre course along the south coast.

WG774 was subsequently to become BAC-221 fitted with the Concorde-type delta wing for tests.

HAWKER HUNTER FI

The beautiful Hawker Hunter FI was issued to No. 54 Squadron in March 1955. Within a few months the Squadron had achieved a very competent aerobatic team which is depicted in this photograph. By September 1955 the FI Hunters had been replaced by more powerful F4s.

The Squadron's blue and yellow chequers are clearly visible on the nose of each Hunter. As with many of the photographs Charles Brown took there was some news event connected with the sequences, in this case it was probably because the team performed at many public air displays that summer.

BLACK ARROWS
In 1957 No. 111 Squadron was nominated as Fighter Command's aerobatic team for which they initially used nine Hawker Hunters. The aircraft were painted black and the team became known as the *Black Arrows.* This photograph was taken by Charles Brown before the SBAC show at Farnborough in 1957.

VICKERS VARSITY
The Vickers Varsity was never one of the most attractive of aeroplanes yet as a postwar replacement for the Wellington X, as a crew trainer, it must have become a very familiar part of RAF life. Charles Brown has captured in this aerial portait the very best aspect of the prototype VX828, set against a beautiful crisp sky. The Varsity made its maiden flight on July 17th 1949, the first deliveries to the RAF began in 1951.

BAC LIGHTNING T4
A remarkable head-on view of XL628, the BAC Lightning T4 which Charles Brown photographed in September 1959.

BLACKBURN NA39 BUCCANEER
The Blackburn NA39, low level, high speed strike aircraft first flew in 1958 at Boscombe Down. The aircraft was capable of delivering a nuclear weapon and would get to its target by being able to fly low under enemy radar defences at speeds in excess of Mach 0.9. As early as 1955 fourteen aircraft were ordered for development flying. Deck landing trials took place on board *HMS Victorious* in June 1959 when the aircraft had been named Buccaneer.

HAWKER HUNTER F4
A Hawker Hunter F4, XF310, with its national markings obscured is photographed carrying Fairey Fireflash, beam riding missiles. This splendid study in light was taken for Fairey Aviation.

PHOTOGRAPHER

Photograph Reference Numbers

The following is a list of the reference numbers of the photographs reproduced in CAMERA ABOVE THE CLOUDS which are held at the RAF Museum.

All enquiries about obtaining prints of these photographs should be addressed to the RAF Museum and not to the publishers.

Page	*Reference*	*Page*	*Reference*
16	P100891	49	Not known
17	5011-11	50	5563-12
18	P100802	51	5779-11
19	5032.7	52	5715-10
20	5011-20	53	5684-3
21	P100790	54	5701-1
22	4728-2	55	5717-3
23	5200-1	55A	5717-8
24	5786-8	56	5793-6
25	5099-4	56A	5793-1
26	5203-13	57	5778-1
27	5457-9	58	5768-5
28	5215-8	59	5814-8
29	5519-9	60	5775-12
30	5500-?	61	5686-11
31	5699-7	62	5686-4
32	5699-3	63	5832-12
33	5509-2	64	5781-2
34	5770-3	65	5582-2
35	5602-5	66	5867-14
36	5510-6	67	5852-4
37	5593-11	68	5846-10
38	5510-16	70	5901/1
39	5582-13	71	5380-11
40	5412-13	72	5904-5
41	5504-1	73	P100325
42	5827-10	74	P100573
43	5412-15	75	P100707
44	5214-17	76	P100606
45	5645-8	77	5909/9
46	5682-6	78	5984-7
47	5762-7	79	5930-10
48	5409-3	80	5915/10

Page	*Reference*	*Page*	*Reference*
81	5925-7	122	6068-3
82	6061-5	123	6101-1
83	5929-1	124	6065-5
84	5953-5	125	6210-5
85	P100360	126	6067-3
86	P100496	127	6127-3
87	5903-9	128	6244-10
88	5960-13	129	6121-3
89	6087-4	130	6075-12
90	6000-7	131	P100395
91	5974-1	132	P100057
92	BRO.9375C	133	6242-4
93	5989-14	134	6115-15
94	5980-2	135	6094-7
95	P100556	136	6084-5
96	P100318	137	6242-10
97	P100482	138	6226-3
98	P100313	139	6329-4
99	P100603	140	6603-1
100	P100521	141	P100203
101	P100153	142	P100283
102	P100233	143	P100437
103	5981-8	144	P100522
104	6087-10	145	6594-8
105	5947-2	146	6622-13
106	5948-1	147	6825-14
107	6025-11	148	6810-14
108	6046-5	149	6519-2
109	6015-1	150	6578-10
110	5936-10	151	Not Known
111	P100157	152	6520-4
112	P100390	153	Not Known
113	P100066	154	6601-3
114	P100548	155	6842-3
115	5982-2	156	6347-4
116	6064-4	157	6811-3
117	6024-5	158	6816-5
118	6125-10	159	6673-9
119	6059-1	160	6123-8
120	5987-8		

The Royal Air Force Museum, Aerodrome Road, Hendon, London.